A Broke Girl's
Bouquet

A Broke Girl's Bouquet

By
Katie Stairs

Printed in the United States of America.
ISBN-13: 979-8-218-46513-1
Photo Credit: Rayah Doniger
Typeset by: Autumn Skye

Scamp Publications
Lutz, Florida

This book is dedicated to my grandparents
who have always stood behind me, fueling
my passion to create and listen to the world.

Table of Contents

White Lilies

Death, Grief, Departure

Served With a Side of Grief

When asked how I would like my eggs
I tell him I want them over easy,
My everyday choice.
It was for innocence, nothing more,
And it wasn't something Death would eat.
It was something to cleanse my soul
From the darkened clouds hanging over.

When asked how I would like my eggs,
I tell him I want them scrambled,
Something mutilated; beaten
With its scraggly form to hide
The lies that bloomed on my lips
Convincing myself you hadn't left.

He asks me if I want cheese
I tell him yes.
For piling on a gooey mesh
Would mask even the deepest wounds
And still manage to hold me together.

When asked how I would like my eggs,
I tell him I want them raw

So I could steal its life
To bring back the soul that withered away
The one that promised me they'd stay
Yet vanished; now gone with the wind.

When asked how I would like my eggs
I tell him I don't want them anymore.
The broken yolk is a mirror of
What I used to see you as
But now you're gone,
Eaten by the recesses of life,
Brought down to drown in death.

Germinate

I tore out my heart and buried it
It was too heavy for me to hold.
So I covered it in dirt
Sprinkled it with green water,
And watched as wasted time grew.

My hopes and dreams diminished
Becoming a sharp darkness.
Where I lay my bones to rest
Let the layers become reeds
And the muscles become vines,
Leaving behind a mess
To cover my footprints.

I suffocate in soil
Letting the dirt cloud my lungs
As roots break up my insides,
Mangling parts of my spine
And tendons to grow flowers
In my place and I create
A garden of wilted grays.

My remains dance with willows
Following them as they weep.
Leaving behind memories
To fill the remaining seeds.

Gibberish

Tongue tied and twisted,
I find words with no meaning
Slipping from my lips.
I trip over commas of spliced thoughts
As I try to mend my statements
Falling into the abyss of my throat.
It's there my voice catches
Making me the fool I feared.

I wish to speak freely
Though the words fumble
And break the sentences.
Because what I mean to say
Isn't quite heard by other ears.
So I will glue my lips together
In hopes to keep my words
From breaking free while
Suffocating the last bits me.

I'm sorry drips from my tongue
As I clear up the skewed
Before sewing the gaps
of my heart to keep it all

from spilling out.
Yet they still trickle pass
And I shiver, holding myself
Knowing, I'll always remain
Tongue tied and twisted.

Butterfly Effect

I picked up the sharp pieces
Of a broken hourglass
The sand slipping past my fingers
Tearing away the soft skin.

I put the pieces back,
Thinking I could undo
The pain that had revealed
Your bleeding fantasy.
I thought I could repair
The sins that covered your skin
But you were already lost.

You had always been
Stuck on a crossroad,
Flying on the back
of a butterfly
That controlled your fate.

I held you with torn petals
But in vain, you fell apart.
Leaving me to stand

In the wreckage of something,
Even superglue couldn't fix.

Nightmare

It felt like a dream,
I had no control over it,
It felt like a dream,
I never had control over it,
Just existing; not knowing who I was,
Where was it exactly?

Falling soundlessly, where was I?
I should have been crying,
Falling soundlessly, where was I?
I had been crying,
My body was numb, I couldn't move.

You were screaming,
A crash could be heard,
You were always screaming,
A crash could be heard,
The scene concludes, I'm out.
It was a nightmare.

Melodic Decomposition

I'm dirt beneath your fingernails,
Teething on the nerves of your cuticles
Infecting the fragile flesh.
Maybe, just maybe
If you'd listened, I'd not be like this
I'm not sorry for that.
My salt breaks down your minerals
Stripping your cells of their skin.
Burning each connection,
Breaking down each sensation
Till there's nothing left.
So no, it seems I'll never be sorry
The cataclysmic melody of my heart
Was too much; it broke your eardrums.
For now, I'll let my body bury yours
Wrapping every part
With what used to be
Soil.

If Only, If Only

Wolf tears drip off broken beaks
For silk soft skies don't live in dead trees
And they never will
Silver fur tangles in feathers still
Revealing the dark fright
Hidden in the moonlight.

Matted skin clings to starved bones
As howls suffocate the unknown;
Bringing in the pain that's bared
By long lost sighs caught in the air.

A full moon rises among the stars
Leaving behind old and worn scars,
Yet the stars are still bleeding
And the wishes are disappearing
Because they can't fall anymore.

That woodpecker can only sigh
While that wolf will only cry
Because "if only" can never be
More than just a hope that flees
Drowned out by the night.

Celestial Love

Hidden in the crevices
Of her glowing skin
There are secrets
For millennia.
And a bright silver glow,
That cuts though darkness,
Drapes the trails that were unknown.
A lonely mistress,
With craters covering her beauty,
Revealing the imperfections
That the sun does not have
And he kills her each rising,
But when she fights back
She strangles his flames
With an eclipse,
Yet it doesn't last forever
And the cycle begins again.

Soulless

Floating in the river of Styx
With a body bound by time
The currents rip her rib cage
Longing for what's lost and
To destroy the boundary
Sketched on by life.

A boat is what carries her
With splinters prodding her skin,
And the spirit's fingers
Tear through her hair
Forever keeping her stranded
In that skewed world of glass.

No Strings Attached

I left it on the coffee table; unstained
But it's too hot, and
You never liked your tea cold.
It was not my fault per-say
Instead, it was your own
You are the claw that rips my skin;
The teeth that gnash against my gums
Causing me to spit the stories
That hid in my retinas.
You brought this on yourself
Not me, because all I can do
Is react, listen, and obey.
There's no one here to save you
You lost your chance years ago
When I broke those glass heels
So the tracks wouldn't lead to you.
You are the one who guides me
Pushes me, kills me, and
At night, when it is too dark to see,
You hold a blade of words to my neck
And cry because you knew along
That the monster wasn't me.

The Seasons Are A-Changin

Her girl stood, hair wrapped in silk
And watched as the world crumbled.
The springly haven falling away
To the grief of winter's snow
For the pomegranate broke her hold.

A daughter raised in innocence
then grew into a heartbreak
Pulled on the seams of his mouth
When it rested upon those red lips.
She had known better than this,
Yet still she sung the chaotic love
Demeter disapproved of.

Oh Hades,
What have you done to my girl?
Now she stands, brown hair tied back,
With black roses painted in hate
Her poor mother left to plea,
Knowing that her only love
Is lost with dying daisies.

Fallen Feathers

White feathers stained red
Where lips held battles
War cries turned to songs
And tears turned to wine.

I was there when crimson spilled,
Watching the silver sword crack
And how bruises had covered
That empty, shivering form.

Hazel eyes dripped with madness
As your smile bled with white,
Sins filled the empty
And the contract signed
Not with faded ink,
But with innocence.

Nothing Left but Water and Ice

You left the taste of blood on my lips
And though the blood was not mine
I still licked it away.
You saved a life only to lose another,
Leaving behind the shell of a man
You used to call yours.
Your body was cradled against mine
And tears fell like a fresh rain,
A lonely rain— your rain.
A heart frozen over,
I felt my lungs constrict
As your own hand betrayed you.
Life fleeing, your last wish was to save me
And though you healed my wounds
That didn't stop my heart from bleeding

Your way was Lit with a Lantern

Your way was lit with a lantern
A fragile light that made many
Tempt to blow you out.
I carried your body to the well
A place we gathered each year
To celebrate the specters' rising.
I watched as you sank down
Deep into the rising waters
We once called home.
Your skin was pale and
Like fog, you seemed incoherent.
Though I still carried your ring
That never let me forget
The knife twisted into my spine
As forgiveness poisoned my nerves
For it was something that need giving
Even though it was your good deeds
That paved my road to hell.

Labels

Hidden behind a shadow
Of what I'm expected to be,
Hidden behind a shadow
Why were you expectant of me?
Those sayings don't match,
Stop trying to compare them.

Truth faded with lies
I scream objection,
Truth faded with lies
I'm choked with rejection,
That piece doesn't fit
So stop forcing it.

Always be proper
A role that is played,
Always be proper
A role that was played,
Burn those old titles
They will not brand me.

Parts of Plight

Picking at the skin
She pulled apart the pieces of her
Face. Steady fingers
Like tools, restlessly
Working the fragile fragments
Until all that's left is gone

The Caged Canary

She sat sipping tea
For once the house was silent
The bed neatly made,
He wouldn't be home
A symphony she could sing,
Without a worry.

Blue Irises

Melancholy, Contemplation

Ex Nihilo, Fragment No.8

You were born from nothing
With hands holding the last
Lumps of light that had trailed
Into the emptiness.

It was just a thought.
An idea that turned
to words and tore through
The seams of the heart
You let them destroy.

Everything that's known
Now lost to your mind
As you became more
Than what you asked for
When you first began.

Now you hold your breath
Let go of those lumps
And with crumpled words
You at last admit
"I was everything."

Springs Lament

It is always at night when
The silence of the darkness slips in.
When my tears turn to pleas
And my heart slips from my ribs.
I watch it sail off
In the wind of what's forgotten
And breathe in the darkness
That had covered it.

I pull ringlets of gold from my head
And they sink into the dreary
I smile…. It is empty.
Shadows hide in the corners
Taunting…tormenting.

Below the surface
There are lungs
Tattered and used,
I listen to them wheeze.
A letter's written in the cells
Of my skin and they let me
Force me—

To consume what is real
And what I will never see again.

Tizzy Tizzy My Little Ditty

Sitting outside my driveway
I rest my chin on my hand and
Watch the neighbor's dog fly,
The same way Gramma did
The day she died.

What was it again?
About those fleas
that Adam had before he left.
It was when your birdies
roosted and I dug chicken shit
From paint-chipped fingernails.
You left me stuck

Humming that old tune
You always sang
About some purple cow
You've never seen,
But you'd rather see than be,
Because getting caught
Meant no more sun-kissed days
In those simmering afternoons.

Now I sit on that memory
Of an old front porch,
Yearning for days
When the ghost of your
Melody didn't haunt me.

As I rock back and forth,
The seeds of my heart rot
Melting those little ditties.
So, I huff away my feelings,
In a puff of what those words
Now leave me to be.

Pantoum for Anxiety

While everyone breathes in, she drowns
Grasping straws with tattered graces
Breaking corners she tries to round
Turning from those jeering faces.

Grasping straws with tattered graces
Torn out guts litter the sidelines
Turning from those jeering faces
Keeping cheeks under the canines.

Torn out guts litter the sidelines
Breaking corners she tries to round
Keeping cheeks under the canines
While everyone breathes in, she drowns.

Bare bones

Opening up is a curse,
One embedded in the chest
Felt in the stomach
And thrown up with ease.

It's childish to wonder
How those fragmented shards
Got me here in the first place.
It was not all me, no it was
Two sides that melted that path,
And how copper words sunk
The ships that left those lips.

So I was left stuck
Buried in the casings of emotion
From something so gone
That it was all lost
The moment I found it.

Little Flickers

Extinguish the fire
It's too dim to see,
And close your eyes,
Feel those words trickle
From your lungs.

You lay on plumes of white
And watch the world go by.
Torn muscles cling to ribs
And your soul decays,
Leaving behind a shell
That wasn't meant to last.

Your wishes fall to rest
On those chains of memory
Ripped by the years of time.
Don't look back;
The emptiness of their cares
Will drown your mind,
And you'll find yourself
Stuck; tattered in a place
You used to call your own.

All Chewed Up

I saw a turtle today
Dead, desolate, and planted
Guarding the shambles of a home.

With a tangerine in hand
I watched the corpse crawl away
Its shriveled head hiding ants
Feasting on the hollowed bones.

My feet are sticky with grief
From the starlight that guided
My path across rose petals,
And yet I have found nothing
But pimples and rotting skin.

The fairness of what's unfair
Ingrains in my saliva
Making my taste buds quiver
Knowing I will lose to death.

So I stick my head in sand
Remember the dead and hide
Within the rays the sun
To print a smile in its cadence.

Malfunction

He loves me, but I do not,
Status update: Facebook blew up.
I don't feel sorry
Because I used to be happy
With a cell phone in hand,
Scouring through pages
Decorated with Hello Kitties
By carefree five-year-olds.

Maybe that's where I got sicker.
Glued to the coffee grinder
Destroying my last organs
But the wires weren't connected
Error: empathy not found.

Where did I go wrong?
Did I not plug myself in
To those street outlets
People usual die for?
It's an answer I'll never know
Hidden in the messy coconut
Swirls of old coffee creamer.

Make note, I wasn't a special girl,
Lonely and old, only
Logging into my computer
With nothing in mind,
But my job to figure out
How pressing tiny buttons
Too small for a mouse to see
Meant something…
But merely was nothing.

No wonder I lift my fingers now
While breathing in the last
Of my worries and letting
out the last of my words.
My mind fills with everything
That used to be before—
ACCOUNT TERMINATED

Lullaby for a Sleepwalker

Quiet settles as she walks
Dancing on the cusp of dreams,
Listen to the way she talks
As she tiptoes on the seams.

Dancing on the cusp of dreams,
A clairvoyant on her path
As she tiptoes on the seams,
Then you see her blooming wrath.
A clairvoyant on her path

Listen to the way she talks
Then you see her blooming wrath,
Quiet settles as she walks.

Within the Desert

In the restless tomb
Of sleep, it's found groveling.
A bitter beast craves
The life that once used to be
Drowned by the drought of its dreams.

Little Lotus Layaway

She sits watching us,
Oh, how jealous she must be
Not to ever feel free.

Orchids

Love, Strength, Beauty

A Songbirds Serenade

If I could, I'd give you the world
Sprinkled with forget-me-nots
Because you deserve the best.

We'll travel through a desert
To the sweetened oasis
To save your parched lips
And kind eyes from doubt
That's been kindred
In your heart.

With matching rings
We brace the world together.
As the wind tears at our hair
And waves nip our toes.
We are Will-O-Wisps
Floating across a sea
Of tender love
And hardships.

I grab your hand in mine
As we both jump

Drifting toward a sky
Filled with ships of dreams.

You, my dear, are the silks of
My web; my constructed comforts
Woven together with the tears
We shed the day our vows
Became reality.

Yes, my love, together we'll rise,
Two pieces on a chess board
Waiting to battle the future.
And we will mend the cracks,
Stitch the fabrics till
Once again, we can sing
A stronger and brighter
"I love you."

Among the Gardens
of My Youth

I remember the days of innocence,
When hasty flowers bloomed
In my grandmother's lullabies.
I, six-years-old, with blonde curls,
Giggled in a fit while wandering around,
Then calling about how I saw something
I knew wasn't there to enjoy stories
Told by the old woman whose hands
Were caked with rich soil.

More laughter would ensue
As fairy wings flapped as loudly
Like a hummingbird's heartbeat.
Mind you the winds were
Strong in those days
When I danced.

I loved to build little homes
From sticks and stones
As my grandmother worked,
But when the lullabies grew louder

I would quiet and plant
Myself among the orchids
And listened to words
That became lost to the garden.

Great-Grannie's Poem

It's hard to think of a world
Without you.
With a heart filled of biscuits,
Each one was kneaded and
Shaped with love.
You made sure not a mouth
Was left empty and tummies were
Stuffed with love, hope, and
The in-between.
It was that little book I'd written,
Where you found brilliance
On each page
Rather than the ramblings of
A blossoming youth.
Your words made my heart shine.
Polished and primed and yet now
There's no words that can
Match how much I miss you.
But you're with me forever.
Through love and carved memory,
You'll walk with me each day
By guiding my path with warmth
With the taste of chicken and dumplings
Permanently on my taste buds.

Elegy for the Owl Lady

Torn wings strewn across the ground,
I find remnants of owl feathers
And watch as they turn to dust.
With a heart ripped open
Tears fell from my eyes
As your home became empty,
Tattered with lost causes
And broken glass.

You held my hands
With the constellations
And helped me paint the sky.
In return I gave you clay dolls
That held stories for centuries, and
I covered you in those owl feathers
Hoping you would fly
And you did...
Without me.

The decay stirs my soul,
With moist dirt under my fingernails
I spread your ashes
Across the dandelions and clovers.

And I watch as the feathers
Fall and lose themselves
In the wind.

The Atlas of the Seas

Her smoothed form sways with the waves
As she sits, bent over, holding the
Weight of the world upon her back.
It seems the sky has cried enough
For she sinks lower each day.
Stone eyes build up coral reefs
And rough limbs conceal the
Life that blooms among the schools
Of fish that gather between her toes.
Maybe her best was enough
To hold both oceans on her shoulders
As her lover carries the planet
Upon each waking day.
Their bond grows stronger
Pushing both of them together.
Her gray curls envelope his body
For he fathers Earth just as much
As she mothers the water of the world.

Ode to the White Wolf

From Buttercups to Dandelions,
They tangle themselves in the white wolf's fur
The song they croon discerns not from lyin'
For they cannot quite place judgment on her.

A child of destiny stands proud and true
Who's blood's brightened chaos melted facade
The white wolf's fate brought him there, right on cue
When Cintra burned and left the girl abroad.

A bond between strangers, shifts, molds, and blooms
With the scent of lilacs and gooseberries
As an air of lovely magic consumes
Aiding to the burden the girl carries.

Maturity comes on to those who seek
But the wolf tripped to it on witch's wing
From longs letters to spoken words, he reaps
Better stories when the bard starts to sing.

A tale recounted throughout the ages
With tragic whimsy from the flower's tongue

Of the lovers wish in crinkled pages
Sealing destiny to always be sung.

Celestial Rising

Oh, our dear mother,
Look how pretty she sit
From a full moon's rise.

Autumn's Beauty

How lovely the leaves fall
In the quiet autumn breeze,
How gently she sings.

Fox's Dream

From a hollowed nook
She watches with vixen eyes,
What sights she must see.

Daisies

Innocence, Hope

Living Mosaic

The body is glass
It's covered in cracks.
The body is glass
It always had cracks.
Each day adds another still,
Till the truth fades from power.

Becoming broken
The pain won't be numbed.
Becoming broken
The pain never numbed.
Slowly dying from the chinks,
Of the diamond heart that broke.

She crumbles within
In nothing but shards.
She crumbles within
She was always shards.
Fighting for fire within,
She will always be living.

Eight Ways to Look at a Clock

I
Seeds held in the hands of life
Past, present, and future,
All concealed in the face.

II
From the chimes of a crying newborn
To the ticks of a mournful crowd,
All wrapped up in the gears of the time bearer.

III
Horologium tells all but knows nothing
For even it can't unlock the secrets,
That have been lost in the black numerals.

IV
A pale hand gently presses against the face
Of the one that is called father time
While the sand of his broken hourglass drips out.

V
Breaking free visions never found in dreams
Of people who had faded into the dark
Shooting out, breaking you by the arms.

VI
Times you have forgotten return
As the hour hand freezes
Letting you relish in your demise.

VII
It's true when you die
Your life flashes before your eyes
Like minutes on a clock repeat.

VIII
Soon it fades, leaving only the old
As your vision turns from joy to pitch,
Those fragile memories forever lost to time.

Glaciem Saltator

A body fashioned in all directions
When it glides across the wind
Filled with the white drops of hope
Of pain; of love.
You were broken free of worry
Holding chaste lips against yours,
Blood pumping, you knew your truth
Satisfaction was what you created
While the ice blended with your toes.
You knew the melody
Words blooming from the curves
Of your arms, your legs, your smile.
Those faults built you up
With the silver composure
You showed off your passions
Allowing color to splatter
On the canvas you knew as
Cold, unforgiving, ice
You held onto his fingers
Nose pressed to his and whispered
Agape; a gentle word
That you knew nothing about
Then you pulled away

Dancing as your body shouted
Eros; showing the world your meaning
placing your name in history
As the lines swallowed you whole.
You offer the one thing you have
Hidden in the nooks of your ribs
You threw out your love
Allowing the world to drown
In what you called yours.

Spring is Here

Honey scents suffocate the air
As her hair dances with the wind
Tangling with the flowers
She grew from her fingertips.

Sweet nectar drips from her pores
As the soil swallows her whole
Allowing her to take root,
And bloom into something beautiful
That was hidden from the world.

Her wings powder her Earth in pollen,
And her eyes grant wishes made
On scattered dandelions.
She watches from her haven,
The dirt sinking into her skin
With petals stitched into her hips.

Springs listens for the life that's born
Growing colors resounding cheer
For her kingdom has returned
And it will never die again.

Elegy to what I used to Be

I am no magician
But if I could turn back time
I would.
Instead, I just stand here
Bloody fingered and-
Holding a broken hourglass
As I watched the Earth crumble.

It was beautiful before then.
With rich flowers in bloom
And trees so tall
I could almost reach the sky.
Though time always changes
And no matter how hard I fight;
No matter how hard I beg
Mother Nature holds no affection
And everything eventually fades.

Yet now in my hand I hold a seed
Fragile like the new snow
Yet warm like a heart.
It's one of her gifts to me
To make up for the past.

A new life, chance
And a change.

Undergrowth

Sow the seeds in soil
Dribble the water droplets
And watch the world bloom.
Its wicker words wash
Away the worries we have
For sunshine brings a new day.

White Roses

Rebirth

Coffee Conversations

Sitting in a coffee shop,
I notice a young woman.
She is tall and lean; except
for the small bump of life that
flourishes from her tummy.
I sigh softly to myself.
My chest aching for something
More than the pain in my heart.

I'm a contorted robot
Making movements less frantic
And careless as a baby.
Maybe I was never real.
A figment taking on the
Life I watch passing me by.
I'm stuck in within a hole of
Bad people I can't call bad.
For my heart still holds them close.

I'll stay angry with the words
And sink into my feelings
While crying each word as they
Get caught in my throat.

The hailstorms will end;
Just give it some time
And I repeat to myself
Goodbye world, hello new life.

Elegy for Growing Up

To grow, we learn the way the world shapes us.
We bury our heads in the pulsing sand
Remembering the reverberations
From when the fruit of our youth had ripen.

It's a bitter whisper we've grown used to.
When the gnawing of daybreak grows too old
We rip through the seams of fresh skin and bone
To soak up the new day with clashing change.

It's the pain in the process that mars us
The scars we carry far beyond our end
While leaving stories behind in our stead
When the words we thought mattered cease to be.

It's in these subtle sounds that we grow sharper
Lessen the regret stewing in our stomachs
Till at last we catch a breath and cry out
"The world's finally ours for the taking."

But the memories of old still settle
In our veins, in the soft, weaker moments

Where they'll try to choke us out with better
More vivid times, but time never will reverse.

No matter how battered our breathing is
We must lay to rest those sweet moments of
Innocence for they'll never be again.
What we know now has replaced what we
Did know; so, we must say our goodbyes and
Completely and entirely march on.

My Time's a-Changin'

I break my back,
My ribs on foxgloves
Translating each lyric
I plant on my wrist
As elegies to my seeds.
I wasn't meant to be,
A simple memory
Forming in the womb
Bursting into the world
With blind wings
And broken bones.
I watch myself bleed
With the songs of Mozart
And I wonder whether
it is nature or self-shame?
A new grave is born
From the ashes of my melodies
So I'll cry till
The poison bleeds out and
I'll shut close that door
That leaked country tunes,
Till my daddy wept.
It's a wonder why life

Has to happen?
But that is a musing
For another day,
Another lifetime
With another me
And new music.

The Colors of a Healing Heart

At thirteen, I first felt it.
The briskness of butterflies
The heat of spring,
A seed was sown, and
 A flower began to blossom.
As the harsh winter wind came,
The green wilted
And the wings clipped
Off those little love bugs.
It was easier back then.
My throat closed up by jitters
each time he neared.
Yet he had turned into it
And it turned into nothing.
Yet those petals still scatter
In the wind, and I watch that
Old flame cackle and flick
with each heartbeat.
I am eighteen now, knowing
I'll never feel it again.

Unsociable Healing

A tap, tap, tapping on my head
Reconnects the brain waves
Stitches back together the neurons
And returns the remnants of my heart
Till I can breathe again.
Those taps are something I believe in.
It bites back the demons
Those monsters, little monsters
Shrivel up as a electromagnetic
Pulse sweep those thoughts away.
A smile lifts on unwavering lips,
Can you see her?
A girl who uses solitude against them.
She's happy, I'm happy.
30,000 pulses later
While the world falls to chaos,
She rebuilds.

Things That Made Me Stronger

A sharp blade thrusted deep into my spine,
A battered brain mending with passing time,
A dissected heart now guarded with fear,
A quiet whisper only I could hear,

My happiest moments tainted with black,
And it's something I shall never get back
The killer of spite who yanks on my chains
Letting me know I won't ever have full reign.

My dreams, my will, my thoughts, life, and heart
All of it now broken and ripped apart
The pills of release; I wanted and yearned
Are too far from me now, or so I've learned.

They day breaks still with clouds of thunder
With nothing more left for me to wonder.
Now I grow from a harden pressures maw
Just watch me, I'll leave them all in awe.

<u>L</u>ever le Masque (Villanelle)

When asked, I wear the mask my sun gave me
For her gracious light soothes my cracked skin–
"You hide all flaws so prying eyes won't see."

It was all for us. That blinding beauty
Shading my cratered cheeks to hide their sin,
When asked, I wear the mask my sun gave me.

Quiet, my silted starlight took a knee
Shoved beneath shadows masking as her win,
"You hide all flaws so prying eyes won't see."

With cycles end, I orbit from her, free
To pull apart her flares cloaking my kin,
But when asked, I wear the mask she gave me.

A pale mistress was all I'd ever be
Yet look at me now; putting my line in.
"Your shine is fleeting: Soon those eyes will see."

What can I say, my chains don't need your key
Those lies let loose with a popped-out pin.

Unasked, I throw off that mask you gave me
"Try and hide my flaws: I'll let them all see."